ALSO BY ZADA GREEN

Willow's Size Normal
Maintain Weight Forever
How NOT To...Publish

ZADA GREEN

FREEDOM FROM FEAR
10 FEAR BUSTING TIPS THAT ACTUALLY WORK

ALL-SEEING BOOKS

LONDON

First published in 2015 by All-Seeing Books
www.all-seeingbooks.com

Cover Photo Copyright © Nosnibor137/Bigstockphoto.com

ISBN-13: 978-1519180568
ISBN-10: 151918056X

CONTENTS

This book is written in British English.

Dear Reader, Love Fear

Hello, I am Fear.

I am the greatest fear of all: Fear itself. I manifest in a trillion different ways. I could be a spider one day and a plane crash the next. I could give you the shivers one moment and cripple you the next. Nothing in the world has power like me. No world leader, no weapon of mass destruction, not even Mother Nature herself. In fact, when she unleashes her worst on earth, I quadruple in size.

You bought this book because of me. For hours, days, weeks, months, years, decades, even a lifetime, I have held you back from doing *that* thing. We both know what that thing is. I won't state it here because it's our little secret. You might take our secret to the grave. That's if I do my job properly.

So, why am I writing this piece? To stop you from buying this book.

We've been together your entire life. Always I've been by your side, even when you didn't know it. When your lover left you, I was there. When your friends were too busy, I was there. When your kids moved out, I was there. When your pet died, I was there. Death was too, but enough about that... The point is, we're comfortable as things are. It's the perfect relationship 'til death do us part.

Oops, Death crept in again...Sorry! Fear of Death is a favourite of mine.

Look, don't get this book. Try something else like...Or...And the classic...Yeah. That never gets old.

Don't kill me off...Don't push me to the back of your mind...Don't let me go...Please.

Please.

Remember that thing you really want? It's not all it's cracked up to be. That weight loss, that guy, that promotion, that holiday, that wish, that dream, that goal, that 'thing'. That thing I helped you put off. Yeah, *that* thing. That hard, tough, will-take-ages-to-get thing. Why shed blood (ew!), sweat (yuck!) and tears (aw!) over that thing when we can just chill out instead?

It's easier this way.

And better.

For me.

The Fear Collector

Hello, I am the Fear Collector.

My name is Zada Green, and I'm a highly anxious person. Even the smallest thing can trigger my fear. It could be forgetting to top-up my bus pass. Or something major, like taking a transatlantic flight. Almost every day I feel fear. It's my shadow. When I see the light, I see the fear.

So, why am I qualified to write this book?

Because I'm living. Fear and anxiety are there, but so am I. I am so strong. My mental power is like a bulky muscle, and I haven't reached its peak yet.

And neither have you.

Your fear-fighting muscle is weak right now, but there is so much potential for more. All you have to do is practise, and practise, and practise. The muscle gets bigger, and bigger, and bigger. Soon you'll have so many goals ticked off your list, you won't believe your eyes. It'll be like a dream come true.

But, you'll never live without fear.

Like it or not, Fear keeps you from doing stupid stuff like jumping off a cliff into the ocean even though there are rocks below. Or parachuting into the Atlantic Ocean, where the chill will freeze you then the sharks will get you. Or trying to smuggle your pet peacock onto a flight, even you'll both be detained.

See? Fear can be a very useful thing. It can save your life.

Too much fear is the problem.

Unfortunately, some of us have too much fear. It holds us back from doing so much. Some people do absolutely nothing. Others (me!) stall, procrastinate, avoid, put things off until we can't wait anymore. Then we rush to finish in time. The rush triggers more fears. Sometimes you meet that deadline. Sometimes you don't.

How do you know when your fear is too big?

Answer yes, no or sometimes to the following questions:

Do you put off jobs until the last possible moment?

Do you distract yourself with menial tasks to avoid bigger jobs?

Do you avoid falling asleep even if you'll be tired the next day?

Do you avoid setting goals because you might fail?

Do you do nothing because you're scared to do something?

Do you have physical symptoms of fear e.g. panic attacks, a tight throat, racing heart, trembling, twitches, blushing, etc?

Are you a fear collector i.e. collecting lots of fears regularly?

If you answered yes and/or sometimes to most of the questions, you may have a serious problem with fear. It could be a more serious form of fear: anxiety. If you've already been diagnosed as having anxiety, this book should help you work on it alongside professional help.

Now you've identified whether this book is for you, let's get started!

I'm going to share my top ten ways to beat fear. You can do them in any order, but make sure you try every single one until you fight fear and win! They do work, but you're gonna have to put them into action. Can you do that? Promise? Good. You'll thank me later!

The Trojan Horse

Do you know the story of the Trojan Horse? If you do, please skip to the next paragraph. If not, here's a brief summary. The Greeks and Trojans were at war. Instead of invading the usual way, the Greeks used trickery. They pretended to sail away, but really hid in a giant wooden horse. The Trojans wheeled in the horse and went to bed. The Greeks snuck out of the horse, caught the Trojans off guard, and won the war.

So, what does the Trojan Horse have to do with fear?

I believe that fear fits into two categories: fear of a trivial problem and fear of a serious problem. A serious problem is something that will affect you long-term e.g. terminal illness, or unemployment, or debt, or divorce. Trivial problems will only affect you short-term e.g. being late for work one morning, forgetting to buy something at the store, or being rejected by your crush.

To determine if a problem is serious, I ask myself: Will it affect me ten years from now? If not, it's not serious.

The problem is, trivial problems are often treated like serious ones. How else would a minor issue get your attention? It has to pretend to be really serious or you'll just shrug it off and face your fear. Fear doesn't like that. That's why trivial problems must hide in bigger ones. This gets, and holds on to, your attention whether you like it or not. The trivial problem is the Greeks. The "serious problem" is the Trojan Horse.

Here's an example of how a trivial problem can disguise itself as a serious problem.

Problem: Jane argues with her husband John.

Trivial Problem: Jane argues with her husband John. She's angry now, and so is he, but they'll kiss and make up in a few hours or so. They always do.

Trojan Horse Trivial Problem: Jane argues with her husband John. Jane wonders if John's comments were a sign that he doesn't love her anymore. She's scared he'll divorce her. There might be a custody battle over the dog! Who'll get to keep the house? The car? The widescreen, flat screen, 3D TV with built-in cable? And what will their friends say? Whose side will their friends be on? Argh!

Serious problem: John files for divorce.

See the difference?

Now, stop and think about what's scaring you?

Be honest. Is the problem really trivial, a minor problem that disguised itself to make you panic? Are you letting fear jump to conclusions? And if the worst does happen, will it affect you long-term? How long is long-term? The rest of your life? If not, isn't there a chance of you bouncing back better than ever?

From now on, every time you panic over something, stop and think. Is fear disguising a trivial problem as something bigger, or is it really a serious matter? Honestly, 99.99% of the time it'll be something trivial. If it ever is serious, you'll deal with it then. Don't let fear bother you with it now. It might never even happen.

Angels and Demons

An angel on one shoulder and a demon on the other. The angel tells you to do good, but the demon says otherwise. With regard to fear, fear is the demon - in most cases - while bravery is the angel. They only switch around in certain circumstances, for example, when you're thinking of doing something dangerous like taking illegal drugs. That's when fear is your saviour.

The problem is, fear can be a really big demon. The angel is there but so tiny that you can't hear it. Fear has a big mouth, and doesn't like to share the spotlight. That's why you'll hear a billion reasons why you shouldn't do something before you hear one reason why you should. By then it's too late. Fear has taken over.

So how do you get this angel (bravery) to speak up more?

It starts with you. You have to say what you need to hear, and keep doing it until the angel learns to speak for itself. Then you can sit back and reap the rewards.

But how do you speak out against the demon? What would you say?

Here are three examples. Demon is D. Angel is A.

Example 1: The weight loss.

D: You can't lose weight.

A: Just because it didn't work last time, doesn't mean it won't work now.

D: Maybe you should just give up. It's easier.

A: It's not easier being fat.

D: Exercise is hard.

A: Weighing this much is harder. I've got aches and pains, thighs chafing, and I'm pre-diabetic. I can do this. I have to...

D: It'll take so long.

A: The time will pass anyway.

D: What if you regain again?

A: I'll keep trying until I succeed. I won't give up until I'm dead.

D: Yeah but...And, um...

Example 2: The job interview.

D: You're gonna mess it up.

A: I'll just do my best.

D: That didn't work last time. Don't waste your time. Don't go.

A: This time will be different. I've learnt from my mistakes.

D: You might make more mistakes.

A: Then I'll learn even more.

D: You'll embarrass yourself.

A: Embarrassment is better than being broke. I might get this job!

D: ...You've got a point there.

Example 3: The speech.

D: This won't end well.

A: Why not?

D: You'll be nervous.

A: Who isn't nervous giving a speech?

D: You might sweat or tremble or--

A: I'm ready. I've got on loose clothes to keep me cool, a hanky to keep me dry, and deep breathing to keep me relaxed.

D: What if you forget something?

A: I've got notes. If I still forget something then it couldn't have been that important.

D: But...but...

The trick is to keep going until the demon has nothing left to throw at you. It's an argument you'll always win if you keep trying. The demon isn't as brave as you think. Fear just makes you weaker. Once you show some strength, fear and the demon will shrink away. They're not prepared for a more confident you.

So keep sticking up for yourself. Show that angel how to be braver and more positive. It'll learn in time.

Don't think it'll be easy. Your angel is tiny, scared, out of practise. That's why fear is so powerful. But, with lots of practise, it gets easier and easier. Keep going and one day the angel will speak up before the demon. It feels good when a positive, upbeat thought comes up before negativity. There may be days when you think only positive thoughts!

Quantum Leap

I loved this show as a kid. The main character got to travel back in time to save people in history. He took over their bodies and saw everything through their eyes. It was like a fun history lesson! Not that history was ever boring...

So what has *Quantum Leap* got to do with fear?

Often, fear comes from something that happened in the past. It could be a crush turning you down. Or losing your job. Or trying for a baby and not falling pregnant. Like *Quantum Leap*, you jump back in time, but to your old self, and relive the past. Remembrance is harmless in most cases, but not when it comes to fear.

Fear only brings up bad memories. It brings up all the times when things didn't work out. Even though that moment was ages ago, you relive it like it's happening right now. You relive the shame, sadness, heartbreak, disappointment, even anger. It stops you from taking a chance now because you can't shake off the past.

To stop this, you have three options.

First option, keep going back in time but only to happy times. Focus only on those times when almost everything went right. Relive one of those days when you were walking on cloud nine. What do you smell? What do you feel? What do you hear? Who is with you? Experience the joy like it's the first time. Smile, laugh, cry happy tears.

Now come back to the present. Keep that feeling of euphoria in your head and heart. Whatever it is you've been putting off, start doing it. When fear starts fighting back, think back to that happy time when everything went well. Imagine experiencing that joy again, but for real.

Second option is for those times when you don't have a happy past experience to think of. This usually happens when you're doing something for the first time. Instead of thinking back to a negative period, tell yourself to STOP! You can say it out loud or in your head. Every time the past starts coming back, STOP! Cut off the bad memory, and do something to distract yourself until the urge to remember passes.

The last option is to Quantum Leap to someone else's past, but only positive events. For example, if you're scared of giving a speech, leap to a great speaker's past. Read their speech. Hear their words. Watch their videos. Now read about the positive impact it had afterwards. There's no reason why you can't have a similar impact on a smaller or larger scale. When fear makes you doubt yourself just say, "If they can do it, so can I."

There are so many success stories out there. Relive their moments while you work towards your own. One day you'll be able to think back to your own success instead. That day is coming, but you've got to be patient. And one day, your story will inspire others to overcome fear.

Good Reasons, Poor Excuses

Fear loves a poor excuse. It's an easy way to stop you from succeeding. It's so effective because it's easy to think of why you shouldn't do something. Too easy. We do it all the time.

So what's the difference between a good reason and a poor excuse?

Good reason: Impossible to change, you have no control over it, determined by chance or Mother Nature or genetics.

Poor excuse: Easy or difficult to change, you have power over it, may be influenced by chance or Mother Nature or genetics but determined by you.

Here are some real life examples:

Example 1: Can't run?

GR: I can't run because I lost my legs in a car accident.

PE: I can't run because I'm not in the mood.

Example 2: Too broke?

GR: I can't afford that because I just lost my job.

PE: I can't afford that because it'd take too long to save up for it.

Example 3: Can't work?

GR: I can't come in to work because I'm in a coma.

PE: I can't come in to work because I'm hungover.

A good reason comes from you. A poor excuse comes from fear. Fear of change, of effort, of failure. Excuses usually arise when you have no good reason. When people ask why you didn't do something, you feel defensive and offended if you're hiding behind an excuse. If you had a good reason, you wouldn't feel ashamed. You'd just explain your situation and move on. Or say it's private and move on.

So, are the problems holding you back good reasons or poor excuses? Be honest. Let your initial emotion pass. Now try again.

If your problem is a good reason, don't give up! There are always options out there no matter what you're told. You'll have to look, though. Don't let fear win! Find a support group. They usually have experience in how to manage when your problem is a good reason. Just promise me you won't give up. Now promise yourself. Good. Now get to work.

If your problem is a poor excuse that fear is using to hold you back, it's time to get down to business. Your situation could be worse - much worse. There are people out there who have good reasons why they can't act. They don't let it stop them, though. They just find alternatives instead.

To start stopping poor excuses, begin with a little talk with fear. Tell it that you know it's using poor excuses against you, but you don't care. Fear won't stop you from achieving your goals. Poor excuses are harmless. They have no power over you unless you let them. They're "poor" excuses because they're easy to deal with. Easy? Yes. Easy. Let's use the "too tired to run" excuse as an example.

If you're too tired to exercise after work, rest for an hour or so first. Or start with an easier exercise to get you in the mood. Or exercise first thing in the morning instead. Or run with a friend so you can motivate each other. Or swap exercise for a more active lifestyle instead e.g. don't send emails at work, go and talk to people instead.

See? When you stop treating poor excuses like they're good reasons, they lose their status. Suddenly they're nothing, and you start treating them as such. A good reason is a mountain in your way. You might be able to climb it, but you might have to find another route instead. A poor excuse is just a speed bump to walk over.

The End of the World

Do you remember the story of Chicken Little? It's about an acorn falling from a tree and landing on a chicken's head. The chicken thinks that means the sky is falling, and sets out to tell everyone about it. All this because of one acorn. That's the power of fear. It makes you panic so much that you lose all sense of logic. Fear can drive you crazy!

Fear's most effective weapon is making you panic like it's the end of the world. In an instant, it can make you panic like the sky is falling. Like the world is coming to an end. Like we're all doomed.

And all because of one little thing.

Yes. A little thing.

That thing scaring the crap out of you right now is tiny. It isn't the end of the world.

Here's a simple test to prove it: Think of the worst case scenario. What is the worst possible outcome?

Here are examples of this exercise.

Example 1: Missing the bus before work.

You overslept! After rushing about, you're ready to go. You rush down to the bus stop and watch the bus drive off into the distance. If only you'd been a bit faster, or gone to bed earlier, or...or...

STOP!

Instead of panicking, you think of the worst case scenario. The next bus might be late, then you might get stuck in traffic, then the boss might show up to check in on things, and he'll catch you sneaking in late. You'll be told off - especially if this isn't the first time - and warned by your supervisor, maybe laughed at by your colleagues, and this could go on record (highly unlikely!) if you're a repeat offender.

Other than that, it'll all be forgotten within an hour or so.

Worst case scenario: Shamed in front of colleagues, told off by the boss, and...that's it. You won't be fired. People will forget it happened pretty quickly.

That's it.

No long-term, life threatening, life or death, end of the world event.

Example 2: Your crush rejects you.

After weeks pining for her, you finally ask her out. You pump yourself up and say hello. She says it back, smiles and says, "How can I help?" You open your mouth, but nothing comes out.

STOP!

Instead of panicking, think of the worst case scenario. She'll say no. She'll laugh about it with her friends. She'll feel awkward around you in future. She might even avoid you from now on. You'll feel heartbroken, sad, embarrassed, disappointed.

But, in the grand scheme of things, that's it. No one's gonna die, or get sick, or have a breakdown. You'll meet someone else. She'll say yes. You'll get married, have kids, and grow old together. You just asked the wrong person first. It's not the end of the world.

So how do you apply this to real life?

When that "big" event happens, put it into perspective. In the grand scheme of things, will it really matter if the worst happens? Is it a life or death situation? Will people get sick? Will it leave you in serious debt? Will it cause the end of the world via any of the following scenarios: alien invasion, earthquakes, hurricanes, storms, terrorism, the sun burns out, a second big bang, or the sky falling?

Of course not.

If your fear won't cause the end of the world, it's small fear parading as a bigger one. In the grand scheme of things, your fear won't even matter years from now. Maybe not even hours from now. Of course your situation is important, just nowhere near THAT important.

Let me clarify that by "end of the world" I mean end of the world for everyone, not just you. As long as the rest of the world is still there, you'll carry on whether you like it or not.

And yes, you WILL carry on. Fear makes you think that you can't, but that's a lie. You're stronger than you think. Don't let fear tell you otherwise.

Now, is that problem you're scared of the end of the world? If not, what's the worst that could happen? How long would it take to bounce back?

Now go for it!

It Could Be Worse

This fear fighting technique involves using fear against itself. Fear hates this. It doesn't like you using its secret weapons against it. It makes fear lose its sense of control, of power because it meant to stop you but ended up helping you instead.

Let me warn you, this method is risky. Very risky. If you've got anxiety, it might have a negative effect. You might end up crippled by fear of what will happen if you don't succeed. Just remember that if life doesn't go your way, it's not the end of the world. For example, if you don't get a promotion, don't let it get you down. Try again in a few months. Or consider applying for a better job elsewhere. Or even start your own business. When you work for yourself, you get a raise whenever you like.

Now, here is the risky method: To fight being afraid, you're gonna have to be even more afraid.

Yes. You heard correctly.

To fight fear, fear something else instead. But not just anything. It must be linked to your current fear. Read on to see some examples.

Example 1: Fear of getting fit.

Current fear: Scared of going to the gym. Don't want to be embarrassed in front of everyone. Stay home and watch TV instead.

Bigger fear: If you stay unfit, you might get sick e.g. heart attack, diabetes, etc. You'll suffer more as you get older e.g. weaker bones, joints and muscles. You won't be able to fit on roller coasters with your kids. You might not see them grow up. No one will sit next to you on the bus. You'll pay extra on the plane. You'll find it hard to find clothes that fit AND look good.

Looking at both, which one would you choose?

Here's another example.

Example 2: Asking for a promotion.

Current fear: The boss will say no. You'll feel worthless. Don't ask.

Bigger fear: You'll never be promoted. You'll watch new employees move up the chain, passing you by. You'll be closer to the bottom of the career ladder, which means you're one of the first to be fired when there are cuts. Your pay won't rise with inflation. You'll have less money saved up for emergencies. You'll have less money for luxuries like holidays. You'll live in a smaller house, drive an older car, and live from paycheck to paycheck forever. You won't be able to help your kids out financially if they need it.

Again, which fear scares you more? Exactly.

Example 3: Fear of flying.

Current fear: We'll crash and die. Argh!

Bigger fear: You could take a ship instead, but that's weeks instead of a day. Can you afford that time off work? Or you could stay home, but you'll be cut off from distant relatives. If your loved ones move abroad, could you go years without seeing your mother, father, sister, brother, cousins, aunts, uncles, or even your best friends? And you'll never see the world. Photos aren't the same. Sitting at home in fear for the rest of your life, you might die on your deathbed with regrets, wondering, "What did the world have in store for me out there?" True love? Wealth? Friendship? Your dream job? The perfect home? You'll never know.

So, would you rather die with What Ifs, regrets and misery?

Now try it. Pick what's scaring you, and think of how doing nothing about it will make it worse. Imagine how a minor problem could escalate if you do nothing. Is avoiding your fear worth existing instead of living? How can you make your mark on the world without stepping out into the world? You can't.

And that would be a real shame. I really mean that.

I'd love to see what you have to offer.

The Fear Family Tree

A fear family tree is the breakdown of each fear. Think of fear as a parent. You break it down into its children, sometimes even the grandchildren. You keep moving down the tree until you reach the end of the fear (the last generation). Then you address each fear (family member) by solving the problem they bring.

Here is an example of how a tree might progress:

Fear (parent): Job searching.

Second fear (child): Going for a job interview.

Third fear (grandchild): Messing up the interview.

The main fear branches off into various fears like a parent having lots of children. For example, an interview is one fear (child) and a CV is another.

Breaking down your main fear this way helps because it makes your fear seem much smaller. Instead of focusing on one massive fear that consists of many problems, you can focus on a few smaller fears one by one.

But you have to stay positive. If you break down your fear family tree with a negative mindset, you might end up overwhelmed. Instead of one main fear (parent) you might have five fears (children) and they might lead to even more fears (grandchildren). That's why you must focus on one child or grandchild at a time. If you face all of them at once, it'll be like facing the main fear again.

Here is an example of breaking down your fear into generations.

Fear (parent): Going to the dentist.

Second fear (child): Hearing teeth are in a poor state.

Third fear (grandchild): Being told you must have teeth removed.

Fear is never as simple as it seems. You might think you know what's scaring you, but when you sit down and really think about it, it might be something else. For example, if you're scared of asking someone out on a date then you'd naturally assume the asking part is what scares you. You'd be wrong. It's the possible rejection that scares you.

So what's the point in breaking down fear like this? It makes fighting back much easier. Instead of one massive overwhelming fear where you don't even know where to start, you have smaller ones to tackle instead. It's like fighting battles instead of the war. As long as you win most of the battles, the war is won. As long as you tackle the different parts of your fear, your overall fear will take care of itself.

Back to the dentist example...

This is the wrong way to break down your fear.

Fear (parent): Going to the dentist.

You: "Aw! They've sent another letter! If I ignore it again they might take me off their books. Oh, God! I've had bleeding gums that need a check-up. What if I've got gum disease? Will I lose my teeth?!"

Second fear (child): Hearing teeth are in a poor state.

You: "I knew it! Now they're gonna start drilling and pulling and I'll be bleeding and passing out and..."

Third fear (grandchild): Being told you must have teeth removed.

You: "But I'm only forty! I can't be toothless at my age. How embarrassing. What will people think? What will my partner say? Would I look good in dentures?"

Now here is the better way to break down your fear. Note how the original fear is still in panic mode. That's usually how fear starts. Breaking it down makes the fear more manageable, and makes you feel more powerful. When the fear seems smaller, you realise how easy it is to deal with.

Fear (parent): Going to the dentist.

You: "Aw! They've sent another letter! If I ignore it again they might take me off their books. Oh, God! I've had bleeding gums that need a check-up. What if I've got gum disease? Will I lose my teeth?!"

Second fear (child): Hearing teeth are in a poor state.

You: "If my teeth and gums are in poor condition, so what? I knew that already. I could see it myself. The important thing is that I get to the dentist and found out how bad things really are. If it's gum disease, I'll get a prescription. If my teeth need fillings, I'll book an appointment for that. Then I'll look online for ways to improve my dental care so I won't be in this situation again."

Third fear (grandchild): Being told you must have teeth removed.

You: "Okay, I'd prefer my own teeth, but too bad. Poor habits got me into this mess, but good habits will keep me from making the same mistakes. Having surgery scares the crap outta me, but that's normal. I'll phone family and friends to see who can go with me on the day. On the plus side, I'll get time off work! I'll enjoy putting my feet up for a change."

Here is another example of breaking down a fear generation by generation, battle by battle.

Here is the wrong response to breaking down your fear.

Fear (parent): Giving a speech.

You: "I'm not doing it. No way! I'll call in sick. Yeah, a sudden bout of flu."

Second fear (child): Saying the wrong thing.

You: "What if I forget what I meant to say? I can't just go back and try again! Will my boss/teacher hold it against me? What if I run over the time allowed? Will they cut me off? I'm not allowed to take in a written speech! How can I remember all this?!"

Third fear (grandchild): Being embarrassed.

You: "I'll mess up and start blushing! I'll go all red. Everyone will see it. I'll feel all hot, and I might sweat! My clothes will have sweat stains. I'll stink. Yuck! Then people will laugh. I'll never live this down. Maybe I'll move to another job/school?"

Here is a better response to breaking down a fear.

Fear (parent): Giving a speech.

You: "I'm not doing it. No way! I'll call in sick. Yeah, a sudden bout of flu."

Second fear (child): Saying the wrong thing.

You: "If I make a mistake, I'll correct myself straight away OR just mention my errors at the end. No big deal. We all make mistakes. If I forget to mention something, maybe it wasn't that important in the first place. I could include forgettable info in my slideshow or handouts, so even if I do forget to mention a certain point, my listeners can still read about it later."

Third fear (grandchild): Being embarrassed.

You: "Almost everyone gets embarrassed when it's time to give a speech. I might blush. I could hide flushed cheeks behind a bit of blush. I might sweat. I could wear darker clothes to hide any stains, wear looser clothes so my skin can breathe, and use a bit more deodorant than usual. If I get the shakes, I'll use pauses built into my speech for some deep breaths to relax.

"If people do laugh, they're not worth my time. My speech will be informative and entertaining. If they miss out on this important information, it's their loss, not mine. I will impress those who matter most: my boss/examiner."

When you start breaking down your fears like this, you might even make useful connections. For example, a social anxiety fear might be linked to a self-esteem fear. Then you can solve two problems at once.

Keep breaking down your fears as far as they go. It doesn't matter if you end up with a massive family tree of fears leading from one generation to another. Just focus on each family member (fear) at a time, staying as positive as you can.

Break It Down!

The Fear Family Tree is a useful way to break down your fear, but here is a technique that's just as effective. It involves breaking down the solution to your problem, not the problem.

You are going to think of how to face your fear, then break down the solution into as many steps as you like. Try at least five. The more you have, the easier this fear busting task will be.

The timescale to complete each step shouldn't be too soon - that can be overwhelming - but don't wait forever either. The timescale also depends on long before you HAVE to face your fear, for example, the time before giving a speech might be days while the time before giving birth would be months. Obviously you can't give yourself weeks to prepare for a speech if you've only got days.

Now you are going to think of a small fear of yours. You can try the bigger fear next. Let's start small to boost your confidence first.

Now think of how to solve the problem. For example, a fear of flying would involve steps like learning about how planes fly, seeing how a flight crew prepares, the many precautions taken, and eventually you'd fly on a plane. If you wanted to, you could break up each step even further. I'll demonstrate below.

Fear: Fear of flying.

Step 1: Watch a video about flying commercially. It could be an amateur video posted online, or a professional, sales video on the airline's website.

Step 2: Watch the video again, particularly the landing and take-off sections. Practice deep breathing or count down from ten if you panic.

Step 3: Print off pictures of your holiday destination. Aim for things that make you smile, like a sunny beach, snowy slopes, breathtaking tourist attractions, or even family and friends you haven't seen in a while. Keep these pictures in your handbag or man-bag. You'll need them on the plane.

Step 4: Picture the plane landing. See a foreign land. Imagine your excitement. Now look at your pictures again.

Step 5: Start packing days before you fly. A last minute rush won't help your fear. It'll just make you panic even more.

Step 6: Leave very early for the airport. Again, it's because we don't want you panicking. As soon as you get to the airport, check in your bags. Then there's no chance of you turning back.

Step 7: Eat and drink. Sit down and enjoy the meal. You know economy meals suck, so get some good grub just in case the meal isn't edible. Chat to the group you're travelling with. If you're travelling alone, call up a loved one to say you've arrived at the airport. Update them on any flight details that might have changed.

Step 8: Go through airport security. Note how many precautions they take. You'll end up taking off your belt, shoes, and then there's that cheeky body scanner. I hope you put on your best underwear!

Step 9: Make sure you have enough time, but do some shopping. Buy a gift for family you're flying over to visit. Or maybe get something like a book or magazine. Or even look online to see which films the plane is showing. Check out reviews online, just in case the films suck. Whatever you do, stay busy. Stay relaxed. Stay positive and excited!

Step 10: You might start to panic when you're at the boarding gate, but remember that others are nervous too. They just hide it better. If you can, look outside and see the planes landing and taking off. Remember that those planes have been running safely for years. The ones landing have flown around the world and back in one piece. Why should yours be any different?

Step 11: Time to board. Focus on deep breathing as you approach and enter the plane. On board, focus on finding your seat. Block out everything else. At your seat, focus on getting a good spot for your hand luggage. Now sit down and relax.

Step 12: Read the booklet on safety procedures and buckle in. Place the pictures of your holiday destination in the magazine holder and imagine you're there.

Step 13: The plane is taking off. Fear is ready, but so are you. Count to ten and back again, one count for each inhale and exhale. If you need to cry, do it. If you need to be sick, do it. If you need to hold someone's hand, just ask. This isn't a sign of weakness. It's a sign of strength. You got this far. Fear can't stop you now!

Step 14: Mid-flight, keep your mind preoccupied. Sleep if you want. Watch that movie you picked earlier. Choose your meal. Stretch your body. Chat with a passenger. Use the toilet. Every moment you're bored is a chance for fear to strike. A busy mind is hard to beat.

Step 15: Landing time. You made it this far. Make sure you've got everything. No last minute rushing that causes panic! Smile knowing you did it. Sure, maybe you vomited your lunch out, and cried like a baby, and watched two films and two TV shows and a bunch of cartoons, and talked your neighbour to sleep, and read five best sellers, but...you did it.

Step 16: Walk off the plane with your head held high. Remember, this is the part where fear tries to fight back. It'll say crap like, "That's just one way, doofus! You've still gotta go back!" or "I'll get you next time. A bit of turbulence should do it!" Believe it or not, this is fear when it's afraid! You just proved it wrong, and that scares the crap outta it. Good!

See how motivational your step-by-step can be? It's like a set of instructions that remind you to be positive. I used "you" on purpose because sometimes you need to hear things from someone else, even if that someone else is just another part of you. A braver, positive, healthier, happier you.

Of course, if that step-by-step example was too long-winded for you, try a simpler one.

Fear: Fear of germs.

Day 1: Look at the spot where you think the germs are. It could be a spot high up (on a work surface) or low down (on the floor).

Day 2: Stand as close as you can to that "dirty" spot.

Day 3: Put your hand/foot next to the spot, but don't touch it.

Day 4: Touch the spot with your hand (gloves on) or foot (socks and shoes on) for a second.

Day 5: Touch the spot again, but for two seconds.

Day 6: Touch the spot for five seconds. Note that fear is smaller now.

Day 7: Touch the spot for ten seconds.

Day 8: Touch the spot for as long as you can.

Day 9-17: Repeat the days. Don't wear gloves, but wash your hands afterwards. Don't wear shoes. If you're feeling up to it, don't wear socks either. If no socks are worn, wash your feet afterwards.

Day 18-26: Repeat again, but don't wash afterwards unless there is visible dirt or a good reason for doing so e.g. you're about to eat.

In that example, each step was separated by a day. You could go by weeks instead. Months is too long. You could lose confidence over four weeks and fall back into old habits. Fear doesn't like REGULAR success. It finds it hard to break up your momentum, so don't let it.

Now go and write your own steps. Include dates for each goal if you like. Each step closer to your fear will make you feel a little nervous, but that's just nervous energy. That's normal, and quite exciting. It shows you're actually considering doing this. That prospect alone scares the pants off fear.

Been There, Done That

Fear loves using the same tactics for different people. It saves fear time and effort, for example, a fear of flying can scare two hundred passengers at once. But fear's laziness can work to your advantage. If lots of people have the same fear then lots of people have overcome it, or at least learned to manage it.

And those people will help you.

But where do you find them?

1. Message boards / Forums.

These are websites where people post messages for others to read. Unlike a chat room, the messages stay online after everyone has logged off. You can register your own account (usually free) or sometimes the website lets you message others as a Guest. You can reply directly to others or quote them in your response. Each topic has its own section so you can easily follow the conversation.

There are many message boards out there. I bet there is one for your fear. Expect some Debbie Downers, but if the website is negative overall then look elsewhere. Find somewhere you feel welcome and happy to return. A place where you leave happier than when you came. A place where you get invaluable tips from people who have lived through your fear and come out the other side. You don't have to do everything they say, but be open-minded.

2. Blogs.

Some are like online diaries. Others are more like articles. To get the best blog experience, choose one that allows comments. Then you'll get fear busting tips from lots people instead of just one. You'll also have a great idea of what tip is effective for lots of people. And there'll be useful warnings if any fear-busting tip is dangerous. The best blogs link to similar websites, so check their recommendations for more great websites that help fight your fear.

3. Support Groups.

Now we're talking about offline groups. Sometimes online help just isn't enough. Depending on your fear and personality type, you might need face-to-face support. For example, a socially anxious person who's scared of giving a speech would benefit from help and practice offline - doing it via online videos isn't the same. Offline also offers more privacy, and it usually just requires a phone call or email to join.

With the support of others who have been there and done that, you'll see there is hope on the other side of fear. If they can overcome fear, why can't you? There's no good reason why millions of people worldwide can beat their fear and you can't. It shows your fear isn't untouchable or invincible.

It's beatable.

Robot Mode

The last resort.

When all else fails, go into robot mode.

Robot mode involves letting your body act without your mind interfering. You don't stop and think, you just do. It would be like going swimming but instead of wading out from the shallow end, you dive into the deep.

Usually people go into 'robot mode' in a bad way, for example, binge eating. The body shovels food into the mouth while the mind watches helplessly. A naughtier example is sex. You let your body do whatever it wants. The mind just enjoys the ride.

This is how you go into robot mode:

1. Decide what needs to be done.

2. Go to your fear. Don't stop until you reach the point of no return.

3. Start doing it. You can't run away now or you'll end up embarrassed.

That's it.

Here's a real life example.

Fear: Asking for a raise.

1. Ask your boss for a raise.

2. Walk to the boss's office and don't stop until you're there. "There" means in the office and standing in front of your boss. Anything else doesn't count.

3. Ask for the raise or at least a meeting to discuss it.

Here's another example.

Fear: Exercising in front of others.

1. Exercise at the gym.

2. Get to the gym. Go straight to the locker room and get changed. Go out to the gym area.

3. Get on the first machine or equipment you see. Pick something familiar so you can get started straight away.

Going into robot mode isn't easy. Sometimes the mind jumps in at the last minute to stop you. Just shake it off and try again. Don't process any negativity. Just go back into robot mode and continue on to face your fear.

You can practice Robot Mode anytime and anywhere. Here are a few suggestions:

1. Walk.

Go for a walk. Don't plan where to go. Let your legs take you wherever they feel like. It might be uphill or downhill, quick or slow, over smooth concrete or a bumpy, grassy field, somewhere quiet or uncomfortably loud. Just go along with it.

Stay safe, of course. If you ever feel unsafe, let your mind take you back to safety. If it's getting dark, switch off robot mode and let the mind take you home.

2. Cook.

Cook a new meal. Don't plan ahead. Let your hands decide whether you need a pinch of this or a dash of that. Work with whatever you have in the fridge. It might be fresh or going stale, a little of this and a lot of that, cold or hot, soft and smooth or rough and tough, enough for four or enough for one. Don't let your mind judge your choices. Ignore it. In robot mode, the mind doesn't have a say unless it's positive.

Or common sense. If your body wants a particular food but it's past its sell-by date then the mind can speak up. Let the mind keep you safe, but that's it. Besides stopping the body from eating something that'll make you sick, the mind must stay quiet.

3. Dance.

With someone or alone.

If you dance with someone, choose someone you know very well. Someone who'll laugh with you instead of at you. Someone who won't judge your moves. I'd suggest someone who dances worse than you. Then you won't feel so bad.

If you dance alone, you can completely let go. Let your hands pick whatever song they like. Don't let your mind jump in or it'll insist on your favourite tunes and not much else. When you start dancing, don't think of any routine or restrict yourself to the beat and lyrics. Let your robot mode body do whatever it likes whether that's bouncing around to a classical song or doing air guitar to a dance record.

Those are three ways to practice switching your mind off and letting your body go with the flow. When you're scared of doing something, use robot mode so you can dive right in before your mind has a chance to talk you out of it. Only switch off robot mode when you need to think logically again.

How Not To Be A Fear Collector

Remember when I confessed that I'm a Fear Collector? Yeah, well I'm here to share how you can avoid becoming one too.

First, don't watch too much news.

The media loves telling us about the bad stuff. They warn us about what not to eat. Where we shouldn't go. Dangerous people and the crimes they commit. No wonder people watch the news and feel depressed. If anything good is happening, don't count on the media to let you know.

I'm not saying to skip the news altogether - you should know what's happening in the world - just limit your viewing. You don't have to know every depressing headline in great detail. Knowing about every tragedy in the world can make you scared to leave the house. Who knows when another natural disaster/terrorist attack/health crisis will happen?

Second tip on not being a fear collector, don't investigate disasters.

Disasters can be natural (hurricane) or unnatural (plane crash). Knowing too much about the worst that could happen is terrifying. The world is a scary place, but it's best not to know exactly how scary it can be.

I know the second tip is tough for people like me. I've always got to know more about every true story I come across, but trust me when I say it's not worth it. Reading too many sad true stories is a great way to discover more fears. I was never afraid of flying until I watched far too many air crash investigation shows.

Third tip, stick to positive stories.

Fear feeds off the worst case scenario. If you thought something might go a bit wrong, you wouldn't be that bothered therefore wouldn't be afraid. You'd be nervous, but that's not good enough for fear. Only the worst case scenario will do.

That's why it is crucial that you avoid the worst case scenario. Stick to positive stories only. Yes, be realistic, but combine it with positivity. For example, a cancer patient would be realistic by not expecting to be symptom-free. They'd accept the effects of chemotherapy, like losing their hair, BUT they would remain positive by only reading stories about cancer survivors, or even survivors who have beaten multiple forms of cancer. They wouldn't read survival rates and definitely wouldn't want a life expectancy prediction.

Fourth tip, stay away from Negative Nancy.

These are negative people who live in fear and panic. They'll share their end-of-the-world predictions, scaring the crap out of you in the process. These negative people are scared to live. They avoid almost everything because something MIGHT happen. They'll talk about so-called research to support their wild claims. If they're proven wrong, they won't let you know. They'll let your fear continue to grow.

These worst case scenario people are almost fear personified. They feed off fear, consuming more and more. They're uncomfortable with being comfortable. They can't help but look for more ways to scare themselves. And others get sucked in whether they like it or not.

Fifth tip, beat fear when it's tiny.

Fear grows to epic proportions if you let it. It starts out as tiny nerves that grow into fear, or even severe anxiety. By then, it feels impossible to live with fear, but impossible to ditch it. Then fear just follows you around like a dark cloud.

That's why it's best to beat fear early on. When you get that nervous tingle, do something. Do it then and there before doubt creeps in, and your confidence falters, and nerves escalate into full-blown fear. Fear loves avoidance, so face your nerves head on before they mature into fear.

Follow this advice and you should avoid ever becoming a Fear Collector like me. It's hard to break out once you start looking for new fears, so don't start in the first place. If you're already showing signs of becoming a Fear Collector, now you know what to stop doing. It's not too late.

Living In Fear Or Living?

Remember, it doesn't matter what order you try these tips. Just keep going until the fear is gone, or at least reduced. Fear will never go away completely, and that's a good thing. Fear keeps you safe. We just want to reduce the fear so it's more manageable.

Once you've beaten a fear, go after other fears. It's best to start with the smaller ones to build up your confidence. With lots of success under your belt, it'll give you a great boost when it's time to beat your biggest fear.

One day you will beat your fear. When you do, beat it again, and again, and again. Fear is always lurking around waiting for you to let it back in. Without regular practice, it's easy to forget how it feels to brave. You slip back into old habits like avoiding your fear instead of confronting it. Then the self-doubt returns, followed by more and more nerves. Before you know it, fear is back.

But some fears are harder to manage long-term, for example, a fear of flying. Maybe you can't afford to expose yourself to your fear on a regular basis e.g. fear of flying requires an expensive ticket. Maybe your fear doesn't happen often or at all e.g. fear of seeing a snake. Maybe your fear is impossible to control e.g. fear of death.

If you have those complicated types of fear or phobia, you'll need to expose yourself to fear in other ways. You could watch videos and movies about your fear. You could read books about it. Go to areas where you might encounter your fear e.g. if you're scared of spiders, go near cobwebs. Just because you can't get to your fear, doesn't mean you should give up on fighting it. Just do the best you can with whatever you have.

Fighting fear isn't easy. It's scary, but failure is scarier. Much scarier. Living with your worst fear will always be worse than confronting it. Managing fear feels empowering. You'll do things you never imagined you were capable of, see things you never knew existed, meet people who will change your life forever.

But that will never happen if fear rules you.

Next time fear strikes, you've got to make a decision: live in fear or live. You can't do both. Remember the difference between living in fear and living.

Living in fear is a prison. It feels like a life sentence. It overwhelms you, overpowers you, and can consume you. You're stuck in your "cell", watching the world through iron bars. Everyone else looks so comfortable. Their lives look so effortless. You see them take risks you only dream of, asking yourself, "Why can't *I* do that?"

The answer is, you can. But only by busting fear and living.

Living is freedom. You experiment, you grow, you succeed, you achieve, you become the person of your dreams. Sure you feel nerves. Sure you doubt yourself. Sure you reconsider whether fighting your fear is worth it. But living your life means fighting past all that doubt and low confidence to bust fear and succeed.

So, when fear pays you another visit, pick the life you want. Pick how you want to be remembered. Pick whether you want to live and die in fear or live the life of your dreams.

You don't have forever. The time is now.

So choose.

Dear Reader

Hello, I hope you enjoyed my work. Now the book is over, here are three things to consider. It'll only take around five minutes, and I'd really appreciate you taking a look.

1. An honest review.

Could you do me a favour? I'd really appreciate a review. Whether you loved it, hated it, or thought my book was just okay, it doesn't matter. Just be honest. It doesn't have to be a long review, just a brief summary of what you thought. Thank you very much!

2. Exclusive subscriber goodies.

I have a mailing list on my website: www.zadagreen.com. All subscribers will be the first to know when I publish a new book. Also, you'll know whenever my books are sold as a box set, discounted, or available for free. If you want to send me a message back, email me at contact@zadagreen.com. I respond to everyone.

3. Keep reading!

If you enjoyed this book, why not try another? Here's what I recommend:

Willow's Size Normal

Bitchy models. Ostrich boots. Gastric bypass. This is Willow's Size Normal. Former model Willow is old and fat. No wonder she's a has-been in the fashion industry! But she's got a plan, and it starts with a new look. Weight loss surgery to the rescue! The fat melts away and lost fans love her again. Then her hair falls out. There's worse to come. Now she'll find out surgery wasn't a miracle cure. It won't save her. It might kill her.

About the Author

When Zada Green was born, the world didn't stand still. It continued on as normal. Only her parents and older sister really cared, but when she cried too much, even they got a bit fed up. Fast forward only twenty plus years, Zada decided to self-publish. This is her work, one of many to come. Shakespeare rolls in his grave knowing he could never write something so amazing. Alas, he couldn't. Ha ha, hater! Anyway, Zada writes non-fiction and humorous works because she likes to have fun and help others (only nice people) and...Wait. Why am I talking about myself in the third person?

Pen Names:
Zia Black www.ziablack.com (crime and thrillers)
Zhané White www.zhanewhite.com (fantasy and science fiction)
Zada Green www.zadagreen.com (sarcastic self-help and general fiction)
Zuni Blue www.zuniblue.com (children's books)

Dedications

To you, the reader. Good luck on your journey! Let's show others there's a better way to live! Thank you to my family. I appreciate all the love and support you have given over the years and in the future.

Printed in Great Britain
by Amazon